THE NEXT TIME WE SAW PARIS

BY

Samuel Hazo

ISBN-13: 978-1-951319-95-3

Cover Design: Jason Price
Cover Image Production: Roy Engelbrecht
Book Interior Design: L. Maltese
Set in Baskerville Typesetting

Printed in the United States of America

Wiseblood Books

CONTENTS

III. TO AIM IN SILENCE

IV. TO RUN OUT OF DESTINATIONS

V. AGAINST UNCERTAINTY

For Mary Anne,
To Sam and Dawn and their three children,
Sam, Anna and Sarah

A few of these poems were published in *Modern Age, Literary Matters, Presence* and *The Pittsburgh Post-Gazette*, but I preferred to retain the rest and not to have them pre-published in journals or other outlets so that they could be read and appreciated first in the context of this book.

ONCE

If once means once, once twice
   is impossible.
         Once is quick
   as a struck match.
         But once
   can be a song that keeps
   singing after it's sung.
Or a poem that's once and always
   at the same time.
         To be complete
   it has to end, but once
   it's over, it begins again.

I. TO BE REMINDED

THE NEXT TIME WE SAW PARIS

"The next time was the last time."

One morning we saw de Gaulle
   himself in uniform chauffeured
   alone in an open Peugeot.
He seemed to dare assassination
   as he did near Notre-Dame
   during the Liberation parade.
On house fronts and doors we noticed
   small bronze plaques with names
   followed by *Victime de Nazis.*
We'd read reports that *Enfants
   des Boches* reached 100,000
   during the Occupation.
                         "Horizontal
   Collaborators" were shorn bald,
   spat upon and marched naked
   through the streets.
                         De Gaulle
   pronounced all executed traitors
   justly punished.
                    We focused
   on Paris of the postcards: Sacré-
   Coeur and the Eiffel Tower.
The Folies-Bergère booked sellouts.
The Bateau Mouches was packed.
Lounging by the Seine, a fisherman
   propped his rod against

a bench and smoked a Gitanes
as if catching a fish meant
little or nothing at all.

Night in the Eye of the Sun

In La Napoule with Mary Anne
  I order mussels steamed
  with aioli, two cappuccinos
  and a warm baguette with butter.
It's almost dusk in La Napoule.
Two waiters are laughing in French
  and folding serviettes.

           We talk
  of Avignon and Aix-en-Provence
  where thousands of sunflowers
  follow the sun to sleep,
  and aisles of lavender look
  truer than they are.

           We say
  if colors can intoxicate, these do
  and then some.

           It's darkening
  in La Napoule.

           We dine
  like partners who have earned
  the ease that work makes possible
  and doubly bountiful because
  it's earned.

           Throughout America,
  where ease means laziness,
  that art is lost.

           In La Napoule
  the night is ours to waste

creatively.

            The buttered crust
of our baguette tastes almost
like the eucharist.

            Tomorrow, fireworks
will celebrate the fall of the Bastille
before the coast grows calm
again.

            The docked and anchored
yachts will mute their lights.
Beach-crews will stack the sunning
mats like so much stock.
The sea that hides more history
than all the oceans in the world
will slow its tides.

            But that
is still a sun away.

            Our private
table feels so much like home
that we forget the time.
It's midnight now in La Napoule.

WHAT SEEMS, WHAT IS

Not that it matters…
                        Skyscrapers
   in Hudson Yards may dwarf
   the desert towers in the emirates.
So what?
            All those who batten
   on irrelevance can feast on that.
Let rocketeers re-name the moon,
   establish malls on Mars
   and conjure floating cities
   in the sky.
               What difference
   will it make to killers in uniform
   who boast of bombs that prophesy
   extinction?
                  If soldiery's the norm,
   then wartime killing will stay
   the alibi for murder.
                        It seems
   unending.
                  As one who thinks
   that love in all its bravery
   can mock the follies of this world,
   I see how disappearance
   lets the unforgettable endure.
What lasts recalls what's lost…
My wife's smile was love
   and bravery combined.

It made
our kind's unkindness something
to defy.
The world is less
without her.
And so am I.

VIGIL

Darkness is illiterate.

                You

  wait for a word, but there's

  nothing.

             You wait for a sound,

  and there's nothing.

                  Midnight's

  a time of its own.

               Whatever

  it hides is yours to imagine.

You almost hear a voice

  you loved above all others.

You'll hear it in your dreams.

But now there's only midnight

  and silence.

             You close your eyes

  and keep them closed, and listen.

THE EYES OF LOVERS

They'll look at each other
    until whatever prompts them
    to keep staring surrenders.
They'll learn that all they ever
    hope to see stays near
    as here but hiding.
              Their eyes
    will fence to a final draw
    that neither even wants
    to win.
          They'll think no more
    of elsewhere or yesterday
    or anything ahead to interrupt
    the marriage of their eyes, mating.

When One Is the Plural of Two

With side-saddling outdated,
   she's post-Victorian.
               She stirrups
   her boots and straddles the saddle.
Off at a gallop, she crouches
   and shortens the reins until
   she and her horse seem one
   and the same.
            It's not for show
   since what she gains in notice
   she loses in grace.
              Result?
A union of talent and action—
   the one perfection we can earn.
It's what can happen when,
   singing, we become the song.
Or when asleep we're suddenly
   awakened from a dream so
   intimate and true that we
   confront the dying world
   like rebels.
           Or least imperfectly
   when love and loving keep us
   nearer and closer and one.

II

What counted for some was numbers.
Mad Jack Donne had mistress
   after mistress before he woke
   and married Margaret.
                     Don
  Juan lost count.
               Casanova
   forgot each woman's name.
Lord Byron scorned his fellow
   poets, swam the Dardanelles
   and proudly philandered at will.
Simenon relieved his boredom
   by playing with a new pair
   of breasts.
            For Romeo and Juliet
   and all who love as they
   loved, who bothers to play
   with numbers?
            One plus one
   is never more than one.

MASCULINE, FEMININE

Men do whatever men
    can do, and that's that.
Later they wonder how
    and why they did it.
                Questions
  arise.
        Being men, they cope.
They make amends.
            Outliving
  their private hells of downs
  and ups, they come to be
  impersonal as nouns…
              Being
  verbs by nature, women
  mock such pantomime.
             For them
  redemption through remorse
  is wiser than regret.
           That's why
  they always seem in action
  even when they rest or sleep.
Paired as a species with men
  like parts of speech, the verbs
  remember what the nouns forget.

CONJUGALS

Each one is the other's only
 other, and so they mate
 without impatience or pretension.
Kisses are their secret language.
Their differences reject what
 difference means whenever
 they embrace.
      They have the gift
 of making imperfections perfect,
 and thoughts of death ignorable.
Parted by necessity or fate,
 they'd feel like amputees.
The fear of that returns them
 to themselves.
      Nothing
 must come between them.
And nothing can or will
 undo their perfect fit.
Together they complete each other
 solely for the need of it.

SENTENCED TO SURVIVAL

The future never happened,
   and the time that should have
   happened vanished on arrival.
The clocks ran backward.
The days were more like nights,
   and the nights were endless.
One life from two was over.
Your days of working, shopping
   for one and waking alone
   returned.
        You came to see
that a life unshared made
living a struggle.
        Dealing
with the curse of dreams recalled
her voice, her touch and all
your ways together.
        Your gratitude
for times you'd suddenly remember
eased the pain but only when
they came without coercion
or remorse.
        Forcing them
back made everything worse.

A Love Like No Other

It happens rarely, if at all.
Age means little.
                    History
        means less.
                    All that matters
        is the mystery.
                    From infancy
        to manhood our son's love
        for his godmother never lessened.
Sixty years between them
        made no difference.
                            For hours
        they could sit in the same room,
        say little or nothing and be
        perfectly happy.
                    Once
        she even let him cut
        her hair…
                    A decade later
        she told my wife during
        their last moments together,
        "A very nice young man
        always comes to see me,
        and he looks just like your son."

GIFTED AT CHRISTMAS

Yesterday morning I ate
   breakfast alone in a restaurant.
A little girl at the next table
   with her grandfather smiled
   at me.
         I smiled back.
              Then
   she ran to my table and placed
   a cellophaned candy cane
   in my hand and said, "For you."
I'm thinking of her now.
It's four in the morning.
             Except
   for a slowly passing car—
   no traffic.
         Out of the night,
   a siren…
         At home alone
   in the dark, I trip on a rug
   below a portrait of my wife.
I blame and damn the rug…
Suddenly a child's smile
   brightens everything around me.
I wonder how she found me.

TO AMIRA WILLIGHAGEN

I listen to a nine-year-old
   Dutch girl singing Puccini
   on stage alone as flawlessly
   as Callas or Netrebko.
Her voice halts me.
              I want
   to word my feelings, but nothing
   happens.
            I have words in surplus
   for the virus-ridden air,
   for cities gone to chaos,
   for soldiers trained for homicide
   in chosen wars.
            But now
I'm wordless.
            Hearing a child
   sing *O Mio Babbino Caro*
   evokes from women and some men
   intelligent tears.
            Applause
   seems insufficient.
            No one
   speaks.
            Like lovers who talk
   after or before but never
   during, they keep to themselves
   the ache of love, happening.

LIFE AT A DISTANCE

We've all been self-imprisoned
    for a week and warned of worse
    to come.
            Robins, finches
    and sparrows peck and perch.
It's sunny but chilly today.
It's pretending to be Spring.
We number six hundred
    Pennsylvanians less than yesterday.
It's even worse in Michigan.
The whole country's a target.
To date there's no defense.
My neighbor's wife stands
    alone on her back porch
    with her dog.
            She waves.
                I wave.

II. TO LIE IN WAIT

SAVED FROM THE SEA

Choppy or calm, the sea
   bothers me.
          It always seems
   to be lying in wait.
             Always.
Before I was six, I fell
   unseen from a dock and was saved
   from drowning by a stranger.
That moment comes to me
   in dreams—the sinking, the saving.
Now I swim well enough
   to save myself, but doubts
   still bother me.
         I never
   relax in the water.
          Never.
Even when I've dared myself
   to swim farther than I should
   and back, the sea still wins.
It never loses.
        It never
   will.
     It never can.

INBRED

Finches arrive in bunches.
They helicopter down and hover
    like hummingbirds before
    they peck in order at the feeder—
each to his ration.
                No one
fights.
        A wild but definite
civility prevails until
each finch is full.
              To share
and share alike is worlds
away from all our public
massacres or wars we wage
for warfare's sake.
               It seems
we are the lone species
that kills its kind by choice.
Lately we've invaded space
and set our sights on Mars.
Will we retain our malice
in the stratosphere and be
as lethal there as here?
              The first
murder on the moon will tell us.

GENESIS

Spurning the fairy tale
   of Eve and Adam, some claim
   we started as one before
   we split in two.
                 If true,
   the split explains what draws us,
   each to each, to be complete.
We're creatures born with groins—
   or loins, if you prefer.
                We keep
   them fig-leafed out of modesty,
   as if ashamed.
              It takes
   an artist to reveal what stays
   concealed so we can see
   how perfectly compatible we are.
Medical charts confirm
   we fork alike below
   our equatorial waists.
We're quick to note the difference.
One has what the other lacks.
One lacks what the other has.
Conceivers persist.
             Receivers
  assist.
      And the split goes on.

All at Once

The once of close calls
in St. Tropez and Saranac—
the once of Kakie's room
with everything in order
down to hairpins—the once
of being told to think
of dying as the "death process"—
the once (if you're lucky or picked)
of knowing that love outlives
both lover and beloved—the once
of a marshmallow swallowed warm—
the once of watching your son
conduct an orchestra—the once
of waiting and waiting and waiting—
the once of seeing that greed
means more than enough
while saving is greed reversed—
the once of baseball or Shakespeare
where time's ignored, and all
that matters is performance—the once
of saying that sin means harming
someone on purpose, including
yourself—the once of wanting
what happened once to happen
once more or never again.

A Picture's Worth a Thousand

Before photography, everything
  was hearsay, transmitted
  by script or printed.
               Cameras
  changed all that.
             Photographers
  became snapshot historians,
  and photographs denied denial.
Capa's photos on D-Day
  recalled what Brady filmed
  at Gettysburg.
         For Duane Michals
  and Helmut Newton, a female
  nude who spurned the shame
  of clothes was naked by choice.
Cartier-Bresson preserved
  what others overlooked.
               Leni
  Riefenstahl made cinematic
  art of Germany's Olympics…
We'd be a different people
  if cameras existed twenty
  centuries ago.
           We still would
  say a Nazarene was crucified.
But who could deny a miracle
  if he was photographed a week
  later risen and walking

with friends to Emmaus?

                       The name

of Paradise Lost would change

to Paradise Found.

                For all

but blind believers, sight

and belief would be the same.

WHEN BEING RUDE SEEMS RIGHT

Whenever he says, "I'm really
  twenty-five, not twenty-six,
  because I was sick for a year,"
  we smile.
               That's just his way.
If he meets someone who says,
  "How do you do," he answers,
  "Do what?"
            Whether asked
or not, he claims, "No one
  visits a rest room to rest."
Unfazed by football millionaires,
  he murmurs, "Boy-men at play
  for pay."
          Regarding fashion?
"Burlesque with a price tag."
His opinion of beards?
               "They hide
  the face."
        Of stubble?
              "Someone
  too lazy to shave."
          Of tattoos?
"Skin-deep doodles."
           On modern
  poetry?
      "Sociology in stanzas."
Mocked and dismissed because

he offends, he says, "Each day
we're here to be offended."
His thoughts on war?

"Everyone
loses."
And peace?

"Really?"
And life?

"It's what we're missing."

THE SERVITUDE

"The pen is a second tongue."

I

Poems come all at once
   or in stages.
               Jealous as love,
   they leave no room for distraction.
A forced poem mimics
   a forced marriage.
                  Failure
   is only a matter of time.
Interrupted, a poem returns
   beyond denial like a love
   that's chosen, conjugal
   and undeniable.
              Similarities
   are obvious even when
   they seem farfetched.
                 Asked
   if he believed in God and why,
   one widower said, "I want
   to see my wife again."

II

To remember wherever you were
   whenever you said whatever
   was heard by whoever was
   with you is just a distraction.

Why do you think there's a past
    to remember?
               Time past is still
    present.
          Time present is passing.
Time future will pass.
              You fret
    like poets who suffer to say
    what they alone can say.
You wait for that moment to come
    the way a male cardinal waits
    for his mate, and she finds him.

WHO?

Recogniton's not the problem,
   but craving recognition is.
Some bet on how they look,
   but banking on looks is fickle.
Consider movie stars long past
   their prime and unremembered.
The same holds true for those
   who make what's private public
   merely for attention.
                    When something
   singular in private becomes
   plural in public, it loses
   all distinction.
            Distinction is what
   all wire-walkers, astronauts,
   strippers and assassins want.
                   Assassins?
Every President's assassin
   but one wanted to be known
   for what he did.
              Oswald
   was blamed for doing what
   was done and then denying that
   he'd done it.
            Murdered before trial,
   he'll always be guilty as charged
   for what he never admitted.
Lone gunman, lone liar or lone
   patsy, he changed a century.

The United *Status* of America

Smoking my pipe, I offered
  Halloween candy to a boy
  who focused on the pipe and asked,
  "What's that?"
              Next—a wedding
  where the bride had the date
  of her marriage tattooed
  on the back of her neck.
                Then—
newscasts ranging from alarm
  to charm.
          Then—cars equipped
  to drive, stop, turn and park
  themselves.
           Then—round-trips
  to the moon for three million per.
Then—tracing ancestries back
  to Adam or part way.
              Then—
students who print their names
because they never were taught
  to write them.
          Then—a third
grader who said that poetry
means "putting your best words
together with feeling in them."
That made up for everything.

SEE HERE

From right honorables to royal
   highnesses we recognize
   their names.
                     Ruling by right
   of vote or sperm, they smile
   and wave.
                     Whether we need them
   or they need us means little
   to us and less to them,
   and nothing to the world.
                     Ice
   in the Arctic continues to shatter
   and melt.
               Nuclear bombs
   stay poised for launch to vaporize
   Boston, New York and half
   of Russia in minutes…
                     Between
   the status quo and Armageddon
   we numb ourselves with spam.
Retirement buyouts promise
   time to travel and loaf.
Vitamins are guaranteed to lengthen
   life equated with arithmetic.
Capsules and plastic surgery
   offer instant adolescence.
Finally, we learn that all
   we have is what is ours

to give.

        Was this what prompted
Mickey to make her cottage
a work of art?

          Or why
Mary Anne chose the perfect
godmother for Sam?

           Or how
Edison saw darkness as the enemy
of light and did something about it?

DESIRE

The French call it an excess
  of health.
           Dante named it
  a beast within us.
                St. Francis
  blamed it on Brother Ass.
Seen as a surplus, a carnivore
  or beast of burden slanders
  desire as just another
  appetite.
          Aristotle claimed
  it could be tamed by moderation.
Mystics and ascetics chose
  denial as the only answer...
After it survives denial,
  it keeps us savage in war,
  suspicious of peace, exultant
  in love, impatient when ill
  but always determined.
              Energy
  becomes its synonym—with death
  its contradiction.
           It wearies us
with deeds and freshens us
  with sleep.
         It lets us rise
  redeemable or damnable,

murderous or generous,
uplifting or disgusting
merely by letting us be.

Worlds Apart

An American billionaire donates
   a miniature sub and flies
   expert engineers to Thailand
   to offer free expertise.
Divers from multiple nations
   volunteer their services
   to save twelve boys and their
   soccer coach trapped
   in a flooded cave for weeks.
Knowing their lives could be
   at risk, they dive regardless.
One dies, but the boys and coach
   are saved...
          Elsewhere?

             Mothers
   stranded in Texas or Mexico
   weep for children sundered
   and lost—assassins gun down
   concert goers or third graders
   with weapons of war—hundreds
   of refugees in flight from Libya
   drown near Sicily—Trumpism
   trumps Trump—Israeli
   snipers near Gaza target
   three unarmed boys
   protesting at the border, killing
   all three, their catch for the day.

THOU SHALT KILL

On D-Day alone ten thousand
died.
      Cemeteries in France
commemorate them, grave
by grave…
      The battle of Tarawa
lasted for seventy-two
hours.
      One thousand
marines were killed or drowned.
Their bodies floated face down
in the tide or sprawled half-buried
in the sand.
      Of four thousand
eight hundred Japanese,
only seventeen survived…
Nations rightly honor
the lost.
      But killing is killing.
When waged for honor and other
deceits, war makes the killing
likelier and lawful.
      Historians
claim that Greece made war
on Troy over a kidnapped wife
named Helen.
      In fact, Helen
welcomed the abduction.

                      Paris
was young and handsome compared
with the braggart she married.
                           Greeks
would fight to save a kidnapped
wife but not one who loved
her abductor.
            They settled instead
for a plausible lie.
               Determined
to trade on the Black Sea
that Troy controlled, the Greeks
knew war was the key but only
if seen as noble.
              Rescuing
Helen of Troy from Troy
is what their cause became…
When dangers widen into wars,
what worked at Troy still works
though Troy is off the map,
and Helen has other names.

               To Stuart Herrington

III. TO AIM IN SILENCE

SHOE HORN

It has the curvature that eases
   ankles into heels until
   each foot feels fitted and shod.
It looks plainer than a spoon,
   but it works.
               It always works.
It could have been what kept
   Samson from limping shoeless
   in Gaza, or Richard from screaming,
   "My shoes, my shoes—a kingdom
   for my shoes," or Babe Ruth
   from circling the bases in socks.
Excuse the play on words...
But serious trivia may not
   be as significant as thought
   when flanked with deeper issues.
Brutus was illegitimate.
               Caesar
   was in fact his father.
               Roman
   families of status conversed
   in Greek.
            When Shakespeare's Caesar
utters, *"Et tu, Brute,"*
just before his son stabs him,
he should have said it in demotic
Greek, not vocative Latin.

MAPLEDOM

Their branches beckon like the arms
   of ballerinas.
                From May to October
   their leaves brighten from burgundy
   to orange to tan.
                In the newsworthy
   world of havoc and other
   distractions, maples create
   no headlines.
                Although they've sieved
   the wind through fifty years
   of war after war where millions
   died for nothing, they tell
   no time except their own.
Here in the land of Oz where
   total extinction is likely,
   the maples offer no defense
   but nonchalant irrelevance.

CHIPMUNKIAN

I

He follows his nose to anything
  that smells edible.
                    He squats
like a catcher, clutches a nut
and munches.
                When he tunnels,
he tunnels for one.
               Never
wasting a step, he knows
exactly what's ahead,
behind, above.
              With cheeks
plumped or slack, he shows
how cheeks can store the not
yet munched.
              Why ask if chipmunks
serve a purpose other
than the perfect way
they munch and store?
                At least
they prove perfection at ground
level or below is possible.

II

Seeing a single chipmunk
  dead, fat or asleep is rare.

They have no time for such.
Right now or what's next
   is all they know.
                Compact
   as a change-purse, they nose
   the ground, glance up, dart left,
   skitter or flex erect.
Dinosaurs have gone to extinction.
Hippos are soon to follow.
Chipmunks foretell how
   the meek shall inherit the earth.

BACKYARD ZOO

Twin foxes today, not quite
   as red as expected, but foxes
   for certain…
               Yesterday a possum
   walked the window ledge,
   leaving paw prints on the glass…
Otherwise the usual: white-tailed
   fawns or young does tripping
   like ballerinas in the grass,
   a male wild turkey splaying
   tail feathers in a fan, groundhogs
   and chipmunks in open stealth,
   a pheasant parading like a king
   with seven queens, a skunk
   protected by the private threat
   of stench, a turtle mimicking
   a soldier's helmet on legs
   and plodding east southeast.
My backyard's home to all.
Roofed from birth, the turtle
   disagrees.
           He has no truer
   home to seek than where
   he is no matter where
   he is or where he goes.
If he gets there, he gets there.
If not, he's there already.

TREES ARE A PARABLE

Even the misshapen retain
  a definite grace.
           Although
  it took decades, a sprouting
  tree in Malahide U-turned
  back into the earth, surfaced
  and grew sideways.
           Willows
  in the wind resemble ballerinas.
Cypresses spire at permanent
  attention.
          However briefly
  magnolias bloom, they're worth
  the wait.
          Oaks, maples, poplars
  and elms obey their calendars.
Cedars that survive in Lebanon
  still glorify the mountains
  of the Lord.
          Thickening, ring
  by ring, from a pinpoint center
  in their trunks is how trees reach
  randomly outward and upward
  and aim in silence at the stars.

Steps and Stones

Her black hair is cut short
  and parted on the right.
                          She's
dancing near the Parthenon
with two men on either side
of her, their hands aligned
on one another's shoulders.
Her feet are speaking fluently
  in Greek.
                Bouzoukis match
  her every step…
                          In fact,
she's dancing on what's left
of the Acropolis—a cemetery
now of crumbled stones
that sleep with history and other
lies.
          Concluding the sirtaki,
  the dancers smile and wave.
The stones foreshadow oldness
  without end.
                      The dancers
  disagree.
              They make their own
  tempo, and there's no debris.

Behind What's Ahead

Ahead becomes behind
too quickly to be understood
except backwards but only
partially and even then
so colored by confusion
that months or years might pass
before the first inklings
of insight tell you that what
you saw or heard was not
what it appeared to be
but something totally different
and at odds with memory itself
like all the altered views
of Kennedy's death from murder
by a lone assassin to covert
execution, theories of Amelia
Earhart's fate, verdicts
on Pacelli's papacy or almost
anything that passes for history
since history is what was thought
to have occurred by those
anointed by themselves to say so
exactly as I'm doing now
for no one's benefit but mine
because my views are no
more credible than those of anyone
who must at last conceed

that what was once ahead
for not that long would stay
both inconclusive and confusing.

VENGEANCE

Married and titled as Lady
   Caroline Lamb, she was twice
   a mother.
                Byron was Lord
   Byron whose hobby was women.
"Mad, bad and dangerous to know,"
   she said of him.
                  "No love
   could be outdone," she added,
   "like one that's felt for the first
   time."
           Their bond was poetry
   and passion.
           To meet him
   in secret she dressed as a boy
   or wore a mask.
             Knowing
   he was clubfooted, she flirted
   and danced with total strangers
   while he watched.
               Not once but twice
   she fought him with a knife before
   she was subdued.
            Repeated
   spats defined them as a pair.
After they spat their last,
   she mailed what she believed
   was all he understood of love—
   two snippets of her pubic hair.

Weddings These Days

I

The bride came to church on a tractor.
The groom and groomsmen
  were filmed helping her board.
The tractor itself resembled
  a semi-tank on treads.
The groom did all the driving
  while his bride sat beside him
  and frowned.
          What everybody
  would always remember
  would be farm machinery driven
  by a groom with more nerve
  than taste.
         The bride never smiled.
Dressed in virginal white
  and wielding a bouquet (since this
  was, after all, *her* wedding), she thought
  this whole charade would vanish
  if she just sat still...
         It stayed.

II

One bride at her wedding chomped on
  loud bubble gum while flouncing
  down the aisle.
        At another,
  the groom wore high-laced

yellow sneakers.
                    At a third,
the bride dallied for an hour
outside the church because
she wanted to be sure.
                    At a fourth
were two who took each other
for better or worse while skydiving
down to Texas.
                    Another two
exchanged self-written vows
with sign language side by side
in divers' apparatus underwater.
The sixth and last was a home
wedding where the groom,
having fainted twice, was married
seated and awake but incoherent.

VERDICT

You wait for politics to wipe
   its nose and wash its hands
   of him, but nothing happens.
You look for help from history.
Then you remember how
   a predecessor won every state
   but one before resigning
   in disgrace.
               Had he won
   Massachusetts, Richard Nixon
   and George Washington would be
   paired in unanimity forever.
You're left to read the dice
   of democracy's crapshoot.
Oratory died with Kennedy.
While defecating, Johnson met
   with Secretaries of State
   and Defense.
             Ronald Reagan
   brought Hollywood to Washington.
The lesser Bush excelled
   in cheerleading.
             No one but Obama
   chose targets for the drones.
Trump's favorite presidential
   color?
         Sunlamp tan.

OUT OF THE BLUE

For years I knew of only
   three Sam Hazo's—my father,
  my son and me.
                  Last year
  my son received an email
  signed Yvonne—from Toulouse.
It was, in a word, affectionate.
He called and asked discreetly
   if I knew an Yvonne in Toulouse.
My answer was a discreet
  but curious no.
              He began
  searching by name and found
  a certain "Hazo, Sam" employed
  by Airbus in Toulouse.
               Rather
  than answer or forward the email,
  he scoured further and found
  throughout France forty-seven
  similar Hazo's.
           Instead of telling
  Yvonne of all these options,
  he thought it best to mention
  only Airbus Sam and let
  the other forty-seven Hazo's
  find their own Yvonnes.

DANCERS

"Prose is to poetry what walking is to dancing."
—Paul Valery

Belly-dancing has more lure
  than grace.
            Jansenized north
of the waist, Irish step-dancers
show that legs have minds
of their own.
            Even if
they try, no couple can look
unhappy or bored while dancing
a polka…
            When Fred Astaire
united tap and ballet
on the ballroom floor, all
we had to do was watch
and listen, and the dancing did
the rest.
            The weightless grace
of every step identified
a generation: Gene Kelly,
James Cagney, Ginger
Rogers, Eleanor Powell
and Cyd Charisse.
                  Each one
has danced and gone.

All
that survives is what they left
on film.
We watch and listen.

SALUTES

To Marilyn, who dedicated her novel
    to her husband and their sons—
    "four wonderful boys."
To Greg, who thanked his directors
    and fellow actors for their praise,
    then turned to his wife and said,
    "Veronique, you're the only girl
    for me—I'll see you later."
To Oscar, who barked a whimper
    and looked his last at me
    before the vet injected.
To Julia, who returned the applause
    of four thousand in the audience
    with a smile, a bow and a wave.
To Sam, who accepted as conductor
    the orchestra's orchid bouquet,
    then walked to where his mother
    was sitting and presented it to her.
To the Marine colonel, who agreed
    when I called the wars in Vietnam
    and Baghdad presidential crimes.
To Kennedy, who spoke in Dublin
    of the fallen boys of Wexford
    with Eamon de Valera watching.
To the woman with a Polish accent,
    who gave me road directions

and said, "You made my day"
when I thanked her in Polish.

To Wanda DeSimone

IV. TO RUN OUT OF DESTINATIONS

THE PAINTERS OF NUDES

Like girls not yet aware
  of what a woman's body
  means, they offered Renoir
  the texture of skin.

           On canvas
they became an old man's dream
  of women playfully nude
  for him alone…

          Picasso's
early nudes look almost
  like cartoons.

        His fans
anointed them "Picassos."
Compared to what he mastered
  in his "Blue Period," they seem
  at best a phase…

          Pearlstein's
nudes appear exhausted.
The only feeling they arouse
  is sympathy…

         Egon Shiele
and Gustav Klimt painted
  like "Peeping Toms."

         The yawning
thighs of their nudes expose
  the hidden orifice of queens.
Drawn to perfection, they qualify
  as art.

Photographed, they'd be
pornography...
Compulsive over
cleanliness, Bonnard's wife
spent hours in a bath tub.
Her husband painted her there
time after time...
Rembrandt
painted Saskia in costume
or naked in bed.
Her expression
stayed the same in both.
Theories are a waste of time.
A woman attracts; a man
reacts.
Art as reaction
says less about the woman,
more about the man.

HELEN OF DUKE

We never met.
            I knew you
only through a book you mailed
to me inscribed.
            You wrote
you married Bevington "just once…
forever."
    A Book and a Love
    Affair tells what that meant.
I learned you read to him
    (at his request) in hospice.
Afterward, you travelled:
    Spain, England, Crete, Kenya,
    France, Tibet, Egypt,
    Brazil, Peru.
                You published
    travel diaries that read
    like Augustine's *Confessions*.
After your crippled son
    chose suicide, you travelled
    even more.
                You came to know
    MacLeish by watching his eyes
    when he spoke, pronounced Reagan's
    optimism nothing but an act
    and joked with cummings over drinks.
When William Carlos Williams
    told you that girls found him

handsomer at sixty than he was
at twenty, you said, "Do you
want to bet?'

The chore of travel
lessened to a bore.

You ran out
of destinations.

You found
television a two-dimensional
fake of a three-dimensional
world.

It lost in depth
what it gained in length and width.
After your mother died,
you wrote, "A better life
is better than death."

Time
past returned as time present,
and your longest journey became
the distance from midnight to morning.

To Helen Bevington

THE FATE OF NOTHING

"The Devil's first trick is his Incognito."
—Denis de Rougemont

Forget the pitchfork, the red
  pajamas and the Satan sideshow.
Save those for Halloween.
What's diabolical reflects
  deficiency.
         When we lack
  courage, the lack is devilish.
If we lack love and let it
  molder into hate, the lack
  is devilish.
        When Omar Khayyam
  said, "I myself am heaven
  and hell," he meant that God
  and fate existed within him.
It's always been like that.
If we resist, we keep
  the devil at bay.
        If we
  succumb, the devil has
  his way with us.
        In case
  you've forgotten, the word *evil*
  hides within the word
  devil.
      It's more than symbolic.
It's literally true and shows

what's mocked us since the world
began.
     Where some see losses,
others see gains.
       Where others
see pleasure, some see pain.
No matter what we see or do,
 we're never certain in advance
 if what we do is right,
 or what we see is true.
What else explains why Abel
 noticed nothing in his brother
 to suggest his killer would be Cain?
By then it was too late
 for anything but hate.
       And fate.

RESPONSES

Trying to define a peninsula,
   one historian settled for
   "almost nearly an island."
Somehow that sounded better
   than the usual…
                    Asked
   how he felt during bouts
   of diarrhea, the boy answered,
   "Like I was sitting on an arrow…"
Ordered to retire after
   having spared his superiors
   the scandal they deserved, he had
   no option but silence.
                  His ongoing
   penance was to pray daily
   for the Jesuit order…
                 Informed
   that his Renault was totaled,
   he heard the medic ask him
   how he felt.
              "Malheureusement bien."
Injured or not, the French
   give irony its due…
Ever the envier, Iago called
   the total embrace of lovers
   "the beast with two backs."
The lovers ignored and pitied him…
"Rhetoric," said Yeats, "is the will

trying to do the work
of the imagination."
                    "Don't send
a poem," John Ciardi warned,
"on a prose errand."
                    "Cruelty,"
noted Thornton Wilder,
"is a failure of the imagination."
All three were speaking differently
alike…
          Wounded by dementia,
a retired linebacker said,
"Anyone who plays for pay
is earning profit for the owners."
Then he said it again
because he forgot he'd said it…
Informed that Cardinal Ottaviani
    opposed his reforms, Pope John
    countered, "If he is telling
    the truth, we should listen."
Ottaviani said nothing more…
Invited to the States after
    receiving the Nobel Prize,
    Wislawa Szymborska politely
    responded, "Madam Szymborska
    will come when she is younger."

"Would You Like to See Where James Joyce is Dead?"

The man who made the offer
   owned a Zurich Verlag
   that published Swiss authors
   in English.
           We taxied together
   to Fluntern Cemetery and walked
   where Joyce, Nora and son Georgio
   are buried near an embedded
   plaque beside a statue
   of Joyce.
           He looks less Irish
   than Swiss or French.
              Totally
   relaxed, he's seated in shirtsleeves
   with a cane slanted beside
   his crossed legs.
           A half-smoked
   cigarette slots between
   his cocked fingers…
           Campaigns
   to re-bury Joyce in Ireland
   clearly contradict his chosen
   exile from an Ireland that was.
Buried near him is Nobel
   Awardee Elias Canetti.
More tourists come for Joyce
   than Canetti.

Excepting *Dubliners*,
a masterpiece, Canetti for me
seems wiser, even in translation.

EPITAPH

Canetti was correct..
              We write
     falsely of death because
     we "lack experience."
                   If truth
     is known only in retrospect,
     then death's unknowable because
     the dead are mute.
                   Meanwhile
     closure changes into myth.
Lives once taken live on
     after they end because
     they never end.
                   Is suffering
     the price we pay for finding
     happiness or simply the sadness
     of gratitude?
                   Death has no mercy,
     and hope is a gift.
                   As for
     an afterlife?
                   Resting
     in peace is death re-born
     as a nap to calm the immature.

Unseen at Sight

Sculptures of men in robes
   or uniforms or mounted on horses
   appear defiantly triumphant.
Sprinkled with droppings, they're still
   commanding.
              King Zeus keeps
   aiming his spear.
              Rodin's
Balzac scowls while Dreyfus
   grips the broken sword
   of his injustice like a cross…
Sculpted nude, the bodies
   of women command in silence.
No crowns or robes.
              No uniforms.
No horses.
          Forever in their prime,
   they wait in stone.
              They know
   their breasts and thighs are whispers
   destined to be overheard.
No longer hidden by clothes,
   they let their bodies speak
   without a gesture or a word.

INCOGNITO

You knew what it would mean
   to me before you helped
   to make it happen.
                     After
   it came without a card
   or signature, you acted surprised.
I asked if there was someone
   I should thank.
                     You said
   the giver would have signed
   the card if thanks were
   expected.
                     Since then I've learned
   that gratitude lasts longer
   than acknowledgement.
                          You're just
   the opposite.
                     You're pleased the most
   when those you love are pleased...
At family gatherings you capture us
   on camera.
                     If not for you,
   the way we think we look
   would be as brief as memories.
The only one who's missing
   from a past your photographs
   preserve for us is you.

BY CHANCE

It seems too minor to mention—
  the day a Frenchman found
  my car-keys in Provence and refused
  a tip.
              "Pour la France," he said
  and smiled…
                    Or how my son
  at seven braved the bees
  to bring me Windex to defend
  myself against them.
                          My thanks?
"Get back inside right now…"
Or Monk who saved his nephew's
  life by giving him his kidney.
"I just need one," he said…
Or how Mary's adopted
  daughter from St. Petersburg
  starred in high school soccer
  and never talked of Russia…
What happens without notice
  or acclaim reminds me how
  a ship that's spotted by a man
  marooned for years but saved
  can almost civilize the sea.

Unforeseeable

For Hatts, long gone, whose son
   in his sixties murdered twice.
For Cheryl, who emailed me
   at ninety because she wanted to.
For May, who faked compliments
   as coyly as she faked condolences.
For Frank, who taught his last class
   without knowing it would be.
For Grace, who said that women
   look older at fifty than men.
For Arthur Miller, who wrote
   America's best play so far.
For Judy, whose voice at seventy
   sounded better than at thirty.
For Anna, who never thought
   she'd have to until she had to.
For Selma, who knew what he was
   but married him anyway.
For Hamed, who asked why we make
   a sport of violence and collision.
For Maura, who wrote a book
   on what women know they know.
For Jean, who claimed that foresight
   at best was hindsight in reverse.
For Fred, who tamed his temper
   by swearing in sign language.
For me, who said we live
   in space but die on time.

WITH NOTHING IN COMMON EXCEPT

You learned best from travel.
I learned best by coming
    home.
           You never missed
    anyone's birthday.
                I had
    to be reminded.
              You planned
    for possibilities.
              I planned
    for nothing but the time
    being.
           You always thought
    of others first.
             I had
    to train myself to do it.
Gossips and braggarts bored you.
You showed me how to ignore them.
I never learned why
    you liked beets or loved
    rhythm more than melody.
No poet but me impressed you
    but not that often.
             Beyond
    politics we favored Kennedy
    because he never forced
    a smile.

All who followed him
faked it.
　　　　We disagreed at times
but never mortally.
　　　　　　For decades
we shared irrelevant differences
to learn that love made
all the difference.
　　　　　　The rest
was trivia—nothing but trivia.

E=MC^2

I think of Luther, Rosa
   Parks, St. Joan of Arc
   and Albert Einstein.
                    Could
   Luther have assumed that saying
   "I can do no more" would launch
   the Reformation?
                 Did Rosa
   Parks foresee that keeping
   her seat in the front of the bus
   would change the South forever?
Who could predict that Joan
   of Arc would rise as the soul
   of France after being cursed
   and burned alive?
               And Albert
   Einstein?
           His perfect equation
   of energy, mass and light
   has nuclearized the world.
The formula is small enough
   to cover with a postage stamp.

THE GOSPEL ACCORDING TO

Unless we feel, we fail
  to remember.
           Those killed in war
  become just names or numbers.
And those who took their lives
  by choice?
         Additional numbers.
Or those who took the paths
  of least resistance?
           More numbers.
If we believe Erasmus,
  the world is ruled by folly.
What passes for honor is folly.
Statues commemorate the least
  noble.
      The infamous and wealthy
  are known eternally by name.
Assassins and saints are buried
  alike in cemeteries groomed
  like gardens.
        The folly of faith
  without love or action sullies
  what passes for religion.
           Entrepreneurs
  and men of state confirm
  Erasmus as a prophet…
           It takes
  a rebel, often a woman,

to choose the option of fools
and live for others.
                    By feeling
what she means and loving how
she lives, she cares for what
is overlooked or lost
and makes what's lasting last.

                    To Janine Bayer

V. AGAINST UNCERTAINTY

THE ODDS

We want what's intimate to last
   as surely as we want the life
   of touch, taste, sight, scent and sound
   to last forever.
             "Tomorrow
I'll be here no longer," Nostradamus
whispered when he died.
Fontenelle near death described
   his fear "…as nothing more
   than trying to go on living."
Dying of fever, Hopkins
   repeated, "I am so happy."
Reactions differ.
             Beliefs
   belie believers.
             All
   that lasts are chosen loves
   and what we hope is hope
   to wage against uncertainty.

ABOUT THE AUTHOR

The author of books of poetry, fiction, essays and plays, Samuel Hazo is the founder and director of the International Poetry Forum in Pittsburgh, Pennsylvania. He is also McAnulty Distinguished Professor of English Emeritus at Duquesne University, where he taught for forty-three years. From 1950 until 1957 he served in the United States Marine Corps, completing his tour as a captain. He earned his Bachelor of Arts degree *magna cum laude* from the University of Notre Dame, a Master of Arts degree from Duquesne University and his doctorate from the University of Pittsburgh.

Some of his previous works are: *When Not Yet Is Now, They Rule the World, Like a Man Gone Mad,* and *Sexes: the Marriage Dialogues* (Poetry); *The Time Remaining, This Part of the World,* and *If Nobody Calls I'm Not Home: The Open Letters of Bim Nakely* (Fiction); *Watching Fire, Watching Rain* and *Tell it to the Marines* (Drama); *The Stroke of a Pen* and *Outspokenly Yours* (Essays); *Smithereened Apart* (Critique of the poetry of Hart Crane); *The Pittsburgh that Stays Within You* (Memoir awarded the 2018 IPPY national bronze citation for creative non-fiction); and *The World Within the Word: Maritain and the Poet* (Critique). His translations include Denis de Rougemont's *The Growl of Deeper Waters,* Nadia Tueni's *Lebanon: Twenty Poems for One Love,* and Adonis' *The Pages of Day and Night.*

In 2003 a selective collection of his poems, *Just Once,* received the Maurice English Poetry Award. He has been awarded twelve honorary doctorates. He was honored with the Griffin Award for Creative Writing from the University of Notre Dame, his alma mater, and was chosen to receive his tenth honorary doctorate from the university in 2008. A National Book Award finalist, he was named Pennsylvania's first State Poet by Governor Robert Casey in 1993, and he served until 2003.

Lightning Source UK Ltd.
Milton Keynes UK
UKHW020624130121
376872UK00011B/1245/J